I'm Not Selling the Farm Today

SQUIRREL SIZE PRESS

An imprint of Squirrel Size Press, Glasgow, KY

elizabethrosehoffmanart@gmail.com

Copyright © 2024 by Carole Baum

Cover Artwork by Elizabeth Hoffman

Print edition: 1st (January 2025)

ISBN: 978-1-958334-05-8

I'M NOT SELLING THE FARM TODAY

Musings of a Widow

In memory of my late husband whose name
was Bob or Jack, depending on whose side of
the family was talking to him.

Poems

Carole Baum

Contents

Widowhood Is . . .

not fixing breakfast for two

not sharing the sunset

not sleeping entwined

      like two old vines

not fighting over how the money should be spent

not turning off the lights to save pennies

not buying everything slightly used

not sleeping entwined like two old vines

      holding each other up

not swimming to a raft and back to see who is faster

not watching the partridge in her nest together

not sharing gossip about old Aunt Suzy

not sleeping entwined like two old vines

      solid against the storm

Triolets for Bob

When first I saw you, I loved your face,
I loved your eyes, your nose, your silly grin,
Its features with my fingers traced.
When first I saw you, I loved your face,

I loved the slow and steady pace
You sought so hard my heart to win.
When first I saw you, I loved your face,
I loved your eyes, your nose, your silly grin.

When first we met, we did not guess
That love would come so deep and strong,
And last so long and stand the test.
When first we met, we did not guess

That love bred out of friendliness
Would safe endure and not go wrong.
When first we met, we did not guess
That love would come so deep and strong.

Spring and Fall

In the spring I watched you as we drove
your eyes raised with hope
to triple crosses that dotted the hills
of West Virginia into Maryland.
Tender grass and budding flowers
winked us along the Interstate.

Your voice was clear and sure,
the old voice I always depended on,
I feel fine, best health I've ever been in
except, of course,
for the tumor.

You cheered your roommate in the
 government hospital
talked knowledgably to nurses,
timed the chemo's effects,
kept the faith, in God, in chemo, in yourself.

That fall, low brown grass
hugged the roadside, panted for refreshment.
We drove past the redbud, its green now
turned yellow
no longer winking
from around each bend.

On the drive home
we stopped at the 'interesting' motel on the hill
where you always wanted to stay.

I thought this was working
I was feeling so good.
Your voice trembled; eyes dropped low.
It was the first lie I heard from your lips.

Winter whispered its desire for you
but autumn carried you away in a blazing light
at midnight.
Angels worked the night shift just for you.

This fall did you see me from high
above the crosses
and redbud leaves
winking at you?

Thief

when Death came for you
I did not expect to feel relief
I did not expect that she would take
your pink cheeks
your warmth
your silly grin

but I should have known

my rival of three long years
she walked with both of us
flirted openly with you
in front of me

you came to know her
to trust her
begged me to call her
Friend

And at last you chose her
went with her willingly
left me here to wonder

why I felt relief
at the yellow of your cheeks
and the frozen sculpture
of your silly grin

A Better Place

Here they come
approach the bier
grab your hand
touch your shoulder.

"So glad you came,"
your mouth forms the words
through wooden teeth,
plastic smile.

I knew him well.
He was a wonderful man.
So sorry for you, but. . .
He's in a Better Place.

"Yes," you repeat,
A Better Place---
no more pain, no more pain,
no more fear.

He fought a good fight.
"Yes, a good fight."
Three years of fighting,
recording every small increase
or decrease
of the tumor.

But now he's in a Better Place.
He did not know
how good it would be.

He's 'up there' – in Heaven
talking to his dad, his mom
playing all the sports he loved,
showing off the healed
scars of his earthly pain.

"He's in a Better Place,"
you whisper for the last time,
then quietly leave,
to return
to the house
 so full
of his empty place.

Taking off the Rings

Tell them I want your dad's ring, she whispered.
And so he did, the son—
now the head of the family—
with the quiet strength
born of the subtle shifting of the mantle.

Softly he made his way to the black-suited men
who waited at the back of the room,
men who wore reverence and discretion
and talked in tones of Bible,
and he whispered her request.

One moved quietly to the bier,
I'll take care of this, he offered.
And, though he turned his back to her
and spread his arms like some dark-winged creature
to shield his work from view,
and though she did not see the instant
 it came free
she felt the burn,
 the sting,
heard a cry from her own finger

Then, she walked outside
pulled off the golden band
that she had worn 'til death did them part,
buried it in her son's hand
 beside his father's
and stepped into the solitary
search for her identity.

16

Last Marathon

strip down, dismantle
tuck away
that which can never

be reassembled

coat, shoes, pictures, trophies
all of you I own
of this physical world

time
       to slow
              the pace

this is a race
I do not want
to win

Resurrection

I thought love died
and buried itself
in the ground
with you.

Then I saw it
rising up before me
resurrection and life

of that which was us
you and me
together.

We *were* one.
Sometimes we died
long before you left,
but mostly we lived
grand and large
in small spaces.

Now the *we* that was *us*
lives on,
and I don't know
what to do with it.

Lifesong
for Bob

Open the photo albums, the worn
strings of memory
that need tuning like my old piano—
this hammer needs new felt, that string is loose.

Sing me the stories, I say,
voices of love, gently,
over and over
tightening the melody
tuning and retuning
the song of the pictures.

But the chords are dissonant
not enough, not enough
something is missing
perhaps the pedals…
dampers of time have muted the sound,

Open the cover, my heart's hands beg,
its eyes wait to see the keys,
ears long to hear
but the lid stays closed
something is missing
the key is lost forever.

So I wait, fingers poised,
this side of the bier
longing to play again
the song that is you.

Life's Schoolhouse

This I've learned--
to make ice cream out of snow
to light candles and read to my babies
through the storm
to pluck a dozen chickens in a day
and pack their fleshy meat in jars
for dumpling dinners in winter's cool

to soothe a baby's cry at midnight
to start a fire in a woodstove
and which wood burns fast and hot
and which endures

I've learned the sound of cicada's castanets at noon
Bob White's measured call and response
at day's end
the thick thud of wild turkeys dropping
from trees at midnight
a heart breaking after a teen-age dance
the crunch of gravel at a car's good-bye

I've learned to drive a truck, a tractor,
a sewing machine
to milk a cow, plow a field, strip tobacco
kill a hog, render lard, cook a country ham,
decorate a cake
coax a kitten from under a house

I've felt a baby's fingers
explore my nose, my teeth, my eyes

his cheek soft upon my own
warm breath of sweetness in his kiss.

I know the delicious warmth of sliding naked
into evening's deep green waters
and the curious coldness
of fresh death

I've learned that married life is not a two-step
but an intricate tango 'til forever comes
and when forever's dance is paused
its melody lingers on, and it is sweet

I've learned to drink my tea on summer's porch
outside the closed doors of formal life
to watch the hummingbird sip nectar from a rose
and listen to God's voice within my heart

Fires

I once knew a man
who built fires
from the different woods he knew
chose each one carefully
for its heat or cool

knew how many logs
of certain size it took
to bake a cake or fry a pie
knew how to bank the fire
at night to keep the embers
holding there

knew how to kindle
love and passion
with equal parts of care
banked them long enough
to last a lifetime
past the day his ashes cooled

Connection

these hands in the soil
sifting, yanking,
tugging out weeds

this connection
this morning reminiscence
pulling at my heart

thinking of you
loving you more deeply
than ever I did while you lived

loving your love of the soil
the walnuts
the dogs, the cows — the
Everything

feeling you so close
digging in this dirt
pulling up your hands
your touch

this connecting with you
in your many gardens

The Lane

That country lane leads
to a home of friends I once knew--
there's the tuft of iris they called *flags*
see it bravely waving through
wild mulberry trees?

The house smiles and I drive in
to the smell of chickens clucking
and sweet corn growing
hundreds of ears of corn—free for the picking
with armfuls of love and laughter
and bore worms and click bugs
for poultry pie with roasting ear suppers.

Around the curve, tobacco's lavender locks
await the barber's cut that sends strength
down its ever-widening green leaves.
I love the pungent fragrance
of tobacco in the field
the cutting, spiking, hanging of Kentucky green
and the sweet perfume of mellow brown leaf
singing from black barns in fall.

The barn's still there, open and calling
I step inside to yesterday
where rafters creak with the weight of scrambling,
young bodies,
shouting, grunting, sweating
filling tier upon tier with heavy burley-feathered
sticks of leaf

while old-timers grin at the grimace
 of the new guy coming face to face
with the wall-eyed, green-horned worm
uninvited passenger from the fields,
wriggly observer of the task.

Over there, the old pear tree sighs with heavy limbs
children used to lighten her loaded arms
fill buckets with the green-gold gems
for Miss Horny, Goldie and Pauline,
gentle, brown-eyed giants whose long pink tongues
curled over piano-key teeth
to lift juicy treasures from tiny pink palms.

Turning back, I lift the gate of good-bye
to this place where once upon a time
spiders stretched a garland fifty feet
from walnut tree to window over morning's dew
then smiled secretly at their art
as women do
who hang their clothes on lines.

Longevity

"A fence lasts three years, a dog three fences, a horse three dogs, and a man three horses." German proverb

A tractor has power
she said

A tractor can pull a loaded farm truck
out of muddy fields
clear paths during a blizzard
pull a wagon of hay to the feed lot
push down trees

A tractor can plow the rich earth
bottom side up
she said
exposing the heart of life
hidden in the roots
laying it out to shrivel and dry

A tractor deserves respect
it can grind things in its mighty gears
crush things beneath its powerful tires

A tractor can be stopped
quite suddenly—
disengaged by the clutch

My husband was a tractor
she said
A woman lasts two tractors.

Help!

O God!
What do I do?
I've run the tractor out of gas.
Only, it's not gas it's diesel fuel.
I know that; you told me all the time.
Diesel is different.
Never mix the two.
Never!

So here I sit
In this tractor seat
Waiting.
What should I do?
Where are you?
Where are your words,
Your instructions,
Your patient impatience
Guiding me?

Why am *I* on this tractor?
This was your job, not mine.
Mine was the housework
Yours, the farm and yard work.
Why the hell did you leave
this work to me?
I am so afraid
I will not do it
Right.

Where are you?

Why so silent?
I need you right now!
If anyone could break through
That Great Divide
I'm pretty sure you could.
You could do anything,
Right?

Silence.

OK. . . I will go to the Source
Of your power, your knowledge
Of all things tractor.

I'm looking down	*staring through tears*
Climbing down	*wiping my eyes with the*
	corner of your farm shirt
Walking	*walking dry-eyed now*
To the house	*to our house you built, board*
	by board
To your office	*your always messy office*
And finding the instruction	
Manual	*who needs you anyway?*

September

In this month I need
a quiet place
away from radio and TV
away from friends
or strangers

some calm place where voices
are sounds without
accent, without inuendo
only assurance
 of life, of peace

so I sit here
alone, not alone
afraid to move, afraid
the hum of the A/C blower blanketing
my thoughts
will vanish and expose what

my heart thought it pumped away long ago
and the world will know the crime
of my continued longing
of grief beyond a year

Widow's Dream

I dreamed I awoke after
you touched me.
I saw your knee,
hard and hairy,

coming toward me
and I laughed
reached out to touch it
like I did your arm

that one time, remember?
We were newlyweds
who dined nightly
on each other's stories.

So delicious was the sound
of your voice, I devoured
your tales and swirled them
around in my night's mind.

"What are you doing with my arm?"
you whispered into my dream one night.
Did you think I was ready
for passionate lovemaking?

But I was in the kitchen
with Mamie Eisenhower
listening to Tiny Tim tiptoeing
through the tulips.

We were fixing pancakes
I reached up to the shelf for the cooking oil.
"I dreamed I was holding a bottle
of Wesson Oil. . . but it's all hairy!"

I had your hairy arm raised
in the air.
I had you.
We kissed
and laughed and
made delicious love.

Last night I awoke and laughed
when I touched
your hairy knee.

And then
I awoke
again.

Widow at the Social Security Office

this small box
virginal white at birth
holds the certificate

of marriage
signed in fine blue script
unlike these shaky lines
of my signature

this testament of life
now yellowed
Alpha and Omega
of my social security

this testament of life
long past climbing mountains,
rafting down white waters
or tent-camping with three kids

holds proof of my right
to claim in solitude
that which is neither
social nor secure

I'm Beginning to Fill the House Now

pushing
past you,
over you

funny how the rooms,
at first
so small

and empty,

have begun
to swell with me

like a pregnancy.
ready for new birth

New Rose

this summer, beetles ate the roses,
the bush leaned forward and wept

its leaves dried, and hard
a time of struggling

the third September without you
death's grief nagged on

bending my body forward in a walk
of those who age without nurture

but on this third anniversary
the worm, the canker in the rose, ceased

this warm September morning
the tiniest bud of crimson

pushes quietly forward
from a tender green shroud,

pushes through the dried,
lifeless stem, in spite of itself

inside the house, my hands fly over
keys, pushing out the story

that could not, would not, leave
the final good-bye of your last day

for eighteen hours that day my hands held yours
'til after midnight when angels came for you

for eighteen hours this day my hands release you
finish, at last, just past the hour of twelve

the new rose sleeps a little this September night
in the morning, shy and bold,

petal by petal, it will wake to new life
in hues of emerald and crimson

I'm Not Selling the Farm Today

I'm not selling the farm today.
Today was a good day.

Today I did not gaze over the fields
where we planted the first strawberry
patch twenty years ago.

I did not cut the asparagus that bolts
 beside the untended bed of turnips
you seeded last fall.

Today I did not make
the blackberry cobbler you like
(from the sweet thorny plants—not the tame ones),
nor strawberry shortcake
fresh, from Bisquik, and the Earli-Glo berries Joy
helped you set.

Today I did not remember the cows,
Boss, Pauline, and Miss Horny,
who lined up against the fence to eat sweet pears
from the children's hands

nor the day the rooster chased our son
'round and 'round the house 'til the mongrel,
Sneaky, *saved my life, Mom!*

I did not think about the time the ducks paraded
single file from the pond to the house
clamoring for evening snacks of gleaned corn

nor scan the sky for signs
of purple martins who might nest
in the made-to-order house
you set up last summer.

Today I did not look at the photos
of Tina's bell pepper patch
you helped her tend so carefully
to earn $500 when she was fifteen,

nor remember the summer of
the "Great Tomato Caper"
with our son's rotten tomato fights,
and the mound of non-breakers in our front yard.

I did not walk past the farm truck remembering
our fame at the Farmer's Market selling
the best sweet corn around,

nor sweat in the tobacco field
cutting and spiking beside you
in the hundred-degree summer sun.

Today, I did not remember
the day you flew the kites with the grandchildren.

Today, I did not watch you read the newspaper
in the yellow hammock under the shade trees.

I did not consider the day we walked down the lane

camera in hand to 'shoot' the bob-white hen you
had found on her nest.

Today, I did not count the thirty-seven years
 of our life together.

Today I did not remember the words
of the male nurse
who went off-duty at 6:00 a.m.
I'll be praying for you and your family
it's going to be a long day.

Today I did not think about
 that last,
long day
six months ago . . .

your labored breaths for eighteen hours. . .
beneath our tears. . .
the children's and mine.

No, I did not cry today.
Today was a good day.

I sold the tractor,
the cultivator and the plow
        but,
            I will not sell the farm

                                    today.

About the Author

 Carole Baum has worn many hats: daughter, sister, carhop, salesperson, wife, mother, student, realtor, teacher, grandmother, widow, writer of memoirs, and, most recently, poet. Along the way she earned a couple college degrees called *Bachelor of Arts* and *Master of Arts,* but she cherishes most her *Degree of Hard Knocks* and title of Grandmother. Currently she lives on a small farm in Kentucky where she and her late husband raised strawberries, cows, ducks, chickens, cats and dogs, and three wonderful children.

Acknowledgments

Special thanks to my family, and especially to granddaughter Elizabeth who encourages, nudges, and sometimes, demands I put my works into her very capable hands and get them printed.

To my poet and writer friends at NDPS (Not Dead Poets Society) and DWG (Dunedin Writers Group) who listen, critique, and push me forward, you all inspire me! Thank you.

www.ingramcontent.com/pod-product-compliance
Lightning Source LLC
Chambersburg PA
CBHW030525130626
46549CB00007B/3106